Insecure Extrovert

Nick J Hennessy

BookLeaf Publishing

India | USA | UK

Presentation by *BookLeaf Publishing*

Web: www.bookleafpub.com

E-mail: info@bookleafpub.com

ISBN : 9789357447102

First edition 2021

Rain

I like the rain
Unlike most others.
I like to stay under the covers,
Sip coffee by the window.
I look outside and feel at ease.
My eggs for breakfast, veal for tea.
When raining cats and dogs all day,
I feel it keeps the blues away.

I'm less inclined to love the sun,
Maybe because I am one
To keep my shirt on at the beach.
With sunshine brings the endless crowds,
And traffic makes my mind weak.

I wonder if people will think I'm insane
And if I'm the only one that prefers rain.

Human in a Squid's Shoes

Today has almost begun
The sky illuminates
Filled with dread of what's to come
Our brains look with our eyes.

Never catching the next breath
A hurry is the norm
To stand still is to misstep
Clocks and watches have wings.

Willed to decompress from days
That roll on to the next
Yet transparent hands can't catch
And breaks intangible.

Today is passing by us
It's not an endless pool
Just sit and watch the sunset
When twilight comes, exhale.

Failed Progress

As I sit here and ruminate about which
Streaming service to click on, I think that bitch
On my left will grab my phone and flick the
switch
Inside my brain. The pain... I gain nothing.
Glitch
In the system. My mind is halved, not enriched.
Could spend an hour in the sun, instead the
kitch-
En wasting sixty seconds at a time.
That's fine.
Rather watch life online than improve mine.

Rabbit Hole

The long night swiftly guides into obscurity
Wishes fulfilled never taste quite as sweet
The morning brings half-closed lids and
impurity
The in-laws that you never get to meet

Early nights become late naps and ruined days
Innocence and laughter can turn to hate
'Recommend' edges closer and further away
Wilt by the minute until you capitulate

The sun is the parents coming home
The sun is the alarm
The moon beckons us but fails
To protect us from harm

@DaSavior69

An anachronistic day in the life of Jesus Christ
He scrolls through Tik Tok where big booty girls
come to life
Exclaims his name in vain and fame's insane as
he's live streaming
The hate from mates, debates with saints and
atheists, demeaning
But before a statement can be formulated by his
reps,
He kills himself from bullying as he is now
depressed.

Three days later he returns, and hesitant he's
become
He's welcomed back with loving arms, after all
he is the one
He then pretends again, defends expending his
time ogling
Says something sympathetic surely still is just
hornswoggling
Our short attention spans forgive quicker than
light scans
Was he forgiven as he is Jesus or as he is a man?

The Fly

A jumping castle after the party.

A Christmas tree in late February.

An engagement ring after the divorce.

A love interest after the perfect date,
But you weren't invited to the restaurant.

Removing protection after the fact,
Yet they didn't get to finish you off.

A past participle has forgotten
What a past participle even means.

A fly on the wall is as pointless as
One that's squashed betwixt a hand and table.
I'm unable to admit I'm the fly.

Look at the stars above

A gift doesn't change things.
It doesn't mean you love
Me, or even know me.
Look at the stars above.

Nobody is special.
There's always another.
But people act the same.
I'm glue and you're rubber.

Being so transparent
Could lead to my demise.
To make things easier,
I tell myself these lies.

K. E. K.

Do it again after so much trauma,
Have to pretend everything is normal.
Does something exist to pierce this armour?
Ingredients for fun, but outcome is awful.

The glass is empty from all the staring,
I couldn't decide how full it was.
I drained the contents, senses blaring,
Content to blaming myself because

I exit the ocean and enter a pool full of sharks,
Keep my eyes closed although I sleep in the
dark.

Rampant Imperfections

Lacking excellence,
Mediocre aplenty,
A background character,
Vague features,
Coast,
Clutter,
Toast and butter,
Pointless numbers,
Lights and reflections,
Rampant imperfections.

Crazy Uncles Now Threatened

I do not dislike you because we disagree.
To clarify, I hate you, and that is a
Strong word, but I mean it with every ounce
Of my being. I am being calm.
Read my mind. Read my palm. Who cares.
Intergenerational.
Old and out of the loop
Is not an excuse.
Beat the dead horse.
What's the word?
You're a...
Cunt.

No Offence

No offence, but I think that if you tried a little harder, then you wouldn't have so much to complain about. Stop scrolling online for three hours a day, and instead give some value to your miserable life. Helping others would be great, but why don't you start with helping yourself? Don't get me wrong, I love to listen to you whinge and whine and whatever. I just can't help but think if you actually gave a shit about something for once, you'd be less depressed and insomnia-ridden, and maybe wouldn't have to drink every night to numb the fact your future has less prospects than my dead cat... What? I said 'no offence'.

But...

You clearly mean the latter half more
Fervently than the former
Whenever you use the word 'but'
I'm likely the ignorer.

Hard for us to communicate
You might as well abscond
"I'm not a racist, but..."
Just stop there and move on.

Sometimes the back end is
Used to dismiss the front
"I kissed him, but I love you."
"I forgive you, but you're a cunt."

A Proud Affair

Everything's gone stale in my relationship with
myself,
I don't know how to spice things up, if anything
can help.
We're already seeing a professional once a
month,
I'm nothing but a dirty book upon the shelf.

I made me laugh at something stupid in the
shower,
And kept my shirt off to feel an immense surge
of power.
I've made strides and now I'm in a proud affair
with me.
If I am a book then I'll check me out every hour.

Me, Chocolate

Catfish are a threat
Could swipe a murderer
Or even worse, I bet
I'll match a pro-liferer
It all culminates
Into a real meeting
I start to ruminate
Worry is my charm depleting
I start to perspire
Feeling a little strange
Your eyes, the fire
And me, chocolate

Read at 9:56pm

Poisoned or left on read?
Stomach knows no difference
Maybe something I said
Should just go to bed
Faking my indifference.

Not checking every minute
I am not distracted
Maybe I should limit
How far I am in it
But I'm so attracted.

Always reply post haste
That perfect smile
Rely on their bad taste
My efforts a waste?
It could be a while.

Must be another
That's holding the heart
That I so desire
In their palm. Aspire
To enhance my part.

Six alerts later, well

It's finally the one
Wish I'd made her swell
She laughed and I said to tell
Me more. Waiting will be fun.

Electricity

When I think about you and me,
I think of electricity.
No keys or lightning strikes needed,
About which I don't feel conceited.
I have no game or history,
Yet I stand here for you to see;
Uneducated, without promise.
Strength doesn't know what strong is,
Unless thrust between me and you.
A platitude's never been so true.

2021: 26 and single

Right
Left
Left
Right
Left
Right
Right
Right
Right
Left
Right
Match
Chat
Silence
Left
Right
Match
Chat
Laughter
Silence
Right
Left
Right
Right
Match

Chat
Laughter
Banter
Date
Kiss
Laughter
Date
Sex
Date
Sex
Sex
Date
Kiss
Silence
Right
Left
Left
Right
Right
Right
Right
Right
Right
Right
Right
Searching
Death

Separation Anxiety

Seems as though we speak different languages,
At least now I know what pain and anguish is.

Signals get crossed, I feel so lost,
I've sold my heart, but what is the cost?
So ice cold, will never defrost.
No growing old with this love of mine.
He doesn't have a sense of time.
Trips to the store feel like days.
He sits by the window, anticipates.

I am the nucleus, the sun, protagonist,
Don't want him to know what pain and anguish
is.

Poem 19

You never know which piece of the puzzle will
be added last
Try adding it first and you'd not go far
It needs the surroundings to make any sense
Otherwise, an odd blue-grey piece of
paperboard.

An eccentric might claim to be fine and be right
Depressed say the same yet cry to sleep at night
Straight shooters tell all but then ignored despite
Still looking for the right spot for this piece.

Going for seconds when you hate the food
Saying you like the meal when untrue
Bingeing as a reward and not feeling regret
Dropped some pieces under the table.

Capoeira classes as a getaway drug
Try to hold hands but wanted a hug
Using a wrench to strike the nail
Perhaps a figure is forming in the corner.

Speaking ill of a boyfriend every day
Preferred than the prospect of lonely disdain
Group delusions are liminal states

The picture is becoming much clearer, now.

A shoulder blade penetrated by steel of the same
name
Less fun it is to confess than to play the blame
game
Harder to open up than hide in the bathroom, oh
Mostly monochromes left, unrewarding.

Once complete, sits proud for just three moons
He now grunts and ignores where once we said
he swoons
The mirror mocks and shames as feelings
untoward
Here I am, left with a stupid picture and 2000
pieces of paperboard.

Chill Pill

If you so wish to know how to be chill,
You must first take the proverbial pill.
I'll give you the ingredients, just give me a sec.
It could be as easy as you do expect.

First you must breathe and count 1, 2, 3,
Then conjure these up: that is my decree.

A sprinkle of swagger can help with the nerves,
Then two cups of phreshness - they act as the
herbs!
You then must put on your most comfortable
clothes,
And get yourself into a comfortable pose.

Touch your nose, flex your toes and then your
confidence grows.
Time slows, front rows and you are one with the
hoes.
(I'm talkin' bout the tool, not the girls with the
butterflies,
Keep paying' attention! Get your mind outta the
gutter guys!)

This is the last thing that you have to do,

Before you stand up to study and say "Screw you!"
Don't think I am tricking. You are not being coerced.
Following this recipe won't make you become worse.

It's simply a tonic to make you more relaxed.
So do what I say, because this is a fact…

Once you have stirred and mixed your large pot,
Do not taste it yet because it's still quite hot.
Add one dash and a half of your favourite liquor,
Now swirl it around quicker, and quicker, and quicker.
Now in slow motion put it into the freezer.
Wait 3 minutes to drink and it will be a pleaser.

Get all of the liquid into a flask,
So it does not taste like arsenic and ass.
Put it under your pillow and on top of your bed,
And fall gently to sleep, just rest your sweet head.

When you awake this flask will be replaced,
With an examination you recently aced.
Your troubles evaporate into the ether,
And leave you a smart, well-adjusted young geezer

Candy

Millionaires' clothes and chandeliers
Could pay the bills for fifty years,
And all the debt of top nations,
Heal the sick, feed starving Haitians,
I could buy my sister a house,
Or build a robot butler that ejaculates candy.